FACT-O-PEDIA

REPTILES, INSECTS AND SPIDERS

MOONSTONE

Published in Moonstone
by Rupa Publications India Pvt. Ltd 2023
7/16, Ansari Road, Daryaganj
New Delhi 110002

Sales centres:
Prayagraj Bengaluru Chennai
Hyderabad Jaipur Kathmandu
Kolkata Mumbai

Copyright © Rupa Publications India Pvt. Ltd 2023

All rights reserved.
No part of this publication may be reproduced, transmitted,
or stored in a retrieval system, in any form or by any means,
electronic, mechanical, photocopying, recording or otherwise,
without the prior permission of the publisher.

P-ISBN: 978-93-5702-281-1
E-ISBN: 978-93-5702-275-0

First impression 2023

10 9 8 7 6 5 4 3 2 1

This book is sold subject to the condition that it shall not,
by way of trade or otherwise, be lent, resold, hired out, or otherwise
circulated, without the publisher's prior consent, in any form of binding
or cover other than that in which it is published.

Contents

Introduction	6
The World of Crocodiles	8
Amazing Alligators	10
Gavialis and Caimans	12
The World of Lizards	14
Colourful Chameleons	16
Iguanas	18
Venomous Lizards	20
Ancient Tuataras	22
The World of Snakes	24
Venomous Snakes	26
Boas and Anacondas	28
Pythons	30
Sea Snakes	32
The World of Tortoises	34
Giant Tortoises	36
Freshwater Turtles	38
Sea Turtles	40
Worm Lizards	42
Glossary	44
Answers	46
Introduction	48
Evolution of Insects and Spiders	50
Habitat	52

Insect Body	54
Life Cycle of Insects	56
Butterflies and Moths	58
Bees	60
Ants	62
Beetles	64
Cockroaches and Termites	66
Crickets, Locusts and Grasshoppers	68
Arachnids	70
Life Cycle of Spiders	72
Spider Webs	74
Tarantulas	76
Unusual Spiders-I	78
Unusual Spiders-II	80
Venomous Spiders	82
Scorpions	84
Glossary	86
Answers	88

REPTILES

Introduction

Reptiles are believed to have originated about 310-320 million years ago. Since then, they have continued to evolve and expand in the world. Reptiles have varying shapes, sizes and structures, but each of them has a scaly body, a head and a tail. Snakes, crocodiles, lizards and tortoises are some of the reptiles that are seen commonly.

Most reptiles are capable of surviving both on land and in water. They have a heart and lungs to breathe. They reproduce by laying eggs and are generally cold-blooded species. Reptiles like tortoises and crocodiles show some of the early traits of the ancient reptiles.

The World of Crocodiles

Crocodiles belong to the group called crocodilians. Alligators, caimans and gavialis (gharials) are also members of this group. The first members of the crocodilian group appeared about 200 million years ago. Researchers have discovered that ancient crocodiles lived strictly on land. However, they gradually started moving towards the water. Modern crocodiles live both on land and in water.

What do they look like?

A long body covered with bony scales characterises crocodiles. They have a triangular snout and huge jaws with sharp teeth. Crocodiles have long muscular tails and webbed feet. Their webbed feet help them swim in the water, while the tail helps them steer the water as they swim.

Saltwater and freshwater crocs

Some crocodiles live in lakes and rivers, while some may live in saltwater habitats such as estuaries and coastal areas. The largest species of crocodiles—the Saltwater crocodile found in Australia—lives in Saltwater habitats.

▲ *A Saltwater crocodile*

Babies

Crocodiles are egg-laying reptiles. A female crocodile can lay 10–60 eggs at a time. It lays eggs in vegetable debris near a riverbank or in the sand. The eggs are hatched by the heat provided by decaying vegetation or the sun. A mother crocodile takes care of her eggs and protects them from predators. In some species, even the father crocodile guards the eggs. Once the babies hatch, the mother carries them to the river where they begin to feed on small crustaceans and insects.

Facts

- The Nile crocodile found in Africa is one of the largest crocodiles. Although its staple food is fish, this huge crocodile may eat larger animals such as zebras and small hippos if they happen to cross its path.
- In 2013, Lolong, the world's largest saltwater crocodile (6.17m), died at the age of 50.

> Which is the largest species of crocodiles and where is it found?

Amazing Alligators

Alligators have been living on Earth for about 245 million years. They are semiaquatic reptiles. They are found only in the United States and China, hence, the names American alligator and Chinese alligator.

Features

Alligators can be recognized by their short U-shaped snout and wide upper jaw. They have a long fat tail and, like crocodiles, they use their tail to propel themselves through water. On land, they can run fast for short distances.

Extreme carnivores

Known for their bone-crushing bites, alligators tend to prey on small animals that they can kill off with a single bite. They usually feed on fish, frogs, snakes, turtles, birds and small mammals. However, they have also been known to attack humans occasionally.

▲ *An American alligator*

American alligators

American alligators are found only in the wetlands of the southeastern United States. They are larger than the Chinese alligators. They are olive, brown, grey, or nearly black in colour with a creamy white belly. They would feel discomfort and would only survive the cold temperature if they submerge their body in the water.

Chinese alligators

Chinese alligators are found only in China. They are relatively smaller in size than the other members of the alligator family. However, unlike American alligators, the eyelids of a Chinese alligator have a bony plate.

Facts

- Alligators can survive for as long as two to three years without eating.
- The tail of an American alligator is nearly half the length of its body.

Babies

The breeding season of alligators is generally restricted to the spring time. A female alligator can lay 30–50 eggs at a time. Alligators are caring parents. A mother alligator builds the nest using rotten vegetation around waterbodies and in wetlands. She guards the eggs after laying them and waits until they hatch. When the babies hatch, she carries them to the water.

How many eggs do female alligators lay at a time?

Gavialis and Caimans

Gavialis (gharials) and caimans are related to crocodiles and alligators. Gavialis are found in the Indian subcontinent, while caimans are found in the wetlands and rivers of Central and South America.

What do Gavialis look like?

One of the largest members of the crocodilian group, a gavial can be easily distinguished by its long snout and narrow jaws lined with razor-sharp teeth. The snout becomes thinner as gavialis grow older.

Gavial diet

Gavialis are incapable of consuming large animals because of their narrow jaws. Young gavialis consume insects, larvae and small frogs, whereas mature gavialis feed on fish only. Some gavialis also feed on decayed animals.

▲ *A gavial*

Features of caimans

Caimans are born with yellow colouring and black spots and bands on their body and tail. An adult caiman has a dark olive-green skin colour. Black caimans, spectacled caimans, broad-snout caimans and smooth-fronted caimans are the various species of caimans. Black caimans, which grow to be about 4.5 m long, are the largest of them all.

Caiman diet

Young caimans feed on insects, crawfish and shrimp. Adult caimans hunt vertebrates such as small fish, reptiles, water birds and amphibians. However, bigger and older caimans may eat larger animals such as wild pigs.

Facts
- Gavialis are the longest living crocodilians.
- Caimans protect their nest from lizards, as lizards tend to destroy them.

▲ *A black caiman*

Spectacled caimans

The spectacled or common caiman is found in saltwater as well as freshwater habitats. These caimans are named for the bony ridge in front of their eyes. The ridge appears to join the eyes together like a pair of spectacles.

Why are gavialis incapable of consuming large animals?

The World of Lizards

Lizards are the largest living group of reptiles. Except for the polar regions, lizards are found in every part of the world. Geckos, chameleons, iguanas and skinks are the different types of lizards. Most lizards are insectivores, while some large lizards may also be carnivores, which may feed on small mammals and birds.

What do they look like?

Lizards have a dry scaly body. They are cold-blooded; thus, their body temperature changes according to their environment. They use their sight to locate their prey as well as to communicate. The majority of lizards have acute colour vision. Lizards are active during the daytime. They use their tail to maintain balance and it also helps them in locomotion. Most lizards have the ability to regenerate their lost tail. They often shed their tails when attacked and grow them back later.

Monitor lizards

Monitor lizards are large carnivorous lizards found in tropical areas around the world. The Komodo dragon and the Crocodile Monitor, two of the largest living lizards, are members of this family. These lizards are usually larger than the other lizards and have longer and strong necks and tails. They have well-developed limbs and long sharp claws. Unlike other lizards, monitor lizards cannot regenerate their tail if it is lost once.

Babies

Most lizards lay eggs. However, some lizards give birth to live young. Some lizards are also known to be ovoviviparous, meaning that they lay eggs inside their own body and then give birth to young ones. Lizards do not make great parents since they do not care for their babies after birth.

Facts

- Komodo dragons can even eat wild buffaloes and humans.
- Some lizards do not have legs.

Which lizard cannot regenerate its tail?

Colourful Chameleons

Known for their ability to change their skin colour, chameleons are members of the lizard family. They are native to Africa, Asia and some European countries. Most chameleons are tree-dwelling, which means that they tend to live in trees and bushes. However, some are terrestrial and live on the ground among leaf litter and low vegetation.

What do they look like?

Unlike most other lizards, chameleons are not small and slender. Their body structure varies greatly in size among different species, the largest being the Malagasy giant chameleon (69.5 cm), and the smallest being the nano-chameleon (1.35 cm).

Most chameleons are heavily ornamented. They have crests, spines and horns. Other typical features of chameleons include eyes that move independently and a long, slender projectile tongue. Chameleons can shoot their tongue to one and a half times the length of their body.

Changing colours

The change in the skin colour of a chameleon takes place due to the presence of chromatophore cells. These cells help to regulate the skin in accordance with the light, temperature and the surrounding environment. It eventually turns out to be a form of camouflage.

What is the other name for Yemen chameleons?

Facts
- Chameleons do not have ears.
- They have a poor sense of smell.

Veiled chameleons

Veiled chameleons, also known as Yemen chameleons, are largely found in the mountains of Yemen, United Arab Emirates and Saudi Arabia. The bony protrusion on their head gave them the name 'veiled chameleons'. These chameleons are green in colour. In males, the green colour changes depending on their emotional state. There are green, yellow, and blue stripes on their body. In female and young chameleons, the green colour is uniform with white marks.

▲ *An African chameleon*

Iguanas

Iguanas have lizard-like bodies and their neck is marked with black, brown or green scales. All iguanas have a flap of loose skin hanging from their throat. They can grow huge, extending up to a length of 1.8 m. They are native to Central and South America and the Caribbean. Apart from these regions, they are found only in Madagascar, Fiji and Tonga.

Green iguanas

Green iguanas are native to Central and South America. They are usually arboreal and herbivorous in nature. They are active during the daytime. Green iguanas are not specifically green in colour. They appear in several colours such as blue, red or orange.

Facts

- The white wig of a marine iguana is the salt that gets collected over its head while it sneezes to expel it from its glands.
- In Central America, iguana meat is called 'bamboo chicken' or 'chicken of the trees'.

Lesser Antillean iguanas

Lesser Antillean iguanas are usually grey in colour. They have large, pale ivory-coloured scales on their head. The young ones of this species are bright green. The population of Lesser Antillean iguanas is on the decline. Several activities such as the destruction of their habitat, hunting, attacks and hybridization with green iguanas have led to their decreasing numbers.

Marine iguanas

Marine iguanas are marine reptiles. They are found only on the Galapagos Islands. These iguanas are very unique. They are the only modern lizards that live and look for food in the sea. Like all reptiles, they are cold-blooded and cannot stay in the cold sea for more than half an hour, after which they return to the shore to bask in the sun.

Where are marine iguanas found?

Venomous Lizards

Gila monsters and beaded lizards are the only two kinds of venomous lizards in the world. They are found in the southwestern states of the USA and Mexico. Their venom is potent enough to kill even a human. They have large teeth in their lower jaw with natural grooves. When they bite, the venom travels through these grooves and enters the body of the victim.

Mexican beaded lizards

The Mexican beaded lizard is one of the four subspecies of beaded lizards, the others being the black beaded lizard, the Rio Fuerte beaded lizard and the Motagua Valley beaded lizard. It is a close relative of the Gila monster and is found in Mexico and southern Guatemala. Mexican beaded lizards, like the other members of their family, have bumpy skin, a thick fleshy tail and short powerful limbs.

▲ *A Mexican beaded lizard*

Gila monsters

Gila monsters are large, slow-moving lizards that may grow up to be 60 cm long. They are usually black in colour, and their body is often marked with various patterns of yellow and orange. These lizards are native to the United States, where they inhabit scrublands, deserts and woodlands. They usually spend most of their time in underground burrows and eat the eggs of birds and other reptiles. They may also feed on small birds, reptiles and insects.

Reticulate and banded

There are two subspecies of Gila monsters—reticulate Gila monsters and banded Gila monsters. In reticulate Gila monsters, the lighter markings form a reticulate pattern, while in the banded, the lighter markings form an unbroken band across the back.

> Which are the two subspecies of Gila monsters?

Facts

- It is wrongly believed that beaded lizards can cause lightning with its tail. Following such superstitions, people kill the lizards in sight.
- A protein found in Gila saliva is used to treat diabetes in humans.

▼ *A pair of Gila monsters*

Ancient Tuataras

Often referred to as 'living fossils', tuataras are one of the most ancient animals on Earth. They are found only in New Zealand and a few offshore islands. Tuataras have been around since the age of the dinosaurs. Most of their relatives died out during the last mass extinction that happened about 65 million years ago. How the tuataras survived, is still a mystery.

What do they look like?

Tuataras are medium-sized reptiles. Their entire body is covered with scales. These scales are more prominent in males. Male tuataras are larger than females. Tuataras have unique teeth. Unlike other reptiles, they have a single row of teeth in the lower jaw, and a double row in the upper jaw. The bottom row fits between both the upper rows when they close their mouth. Tuataras have a third eye on the top of their head. It is also known as the parietal eye, pineal organ or median eye. This eye is visible only in young tuataras and becomes opaque as they mature.

Reproduction

The process of reproduction is slow in tuataras. They are capable of reproducing at an older age. They reproduce once in four years. The eggs of these reptiles are very soft. The incubation period is about 12–15 months. The sex of the egg depends on the temperature around it. Warm temperatures result in males, and cooler temperatures produce female babies.

▼ *A young tuatara*

Behaviour

Tuataras are nocturnal in nature. However, they often come out at the mouth of their burrows to bask in the daylight. They live in cool places because high temperatures are fatal to them. They have a low body temperature as compared to other reptiles. Though tuataras can make their burrows, sometimes they occupy those built by seabirds inhabiting the region.

How often do female tuataras reproduce?

Facts

- Tuataras can hold their breath for as long as an hour.
- Most tuataras live for 60 years or more.

The World of Snakes

Often appearing like a rope, snakes are long, slimy reptiles with flexible bodies. They are both poisonous and non-poisonous. They have different skin colours marked with various shapes and patterns. Although snakes are found in most parts of the world, the majority of them are found in tropical regions.

Babies

Snakes reproduce either by laying eggs or by giving birth to young ones, depending on the species. An adult snake can give birth to 100 young ones or lay 100 eggs at a time. Most snakes do not nurture the young ones. Some are, however, known to build nests and take care of the eggs until they hatch.

Moulting

Like many other animals, snakes shed their old skin for a new one, a process defined as moulting. They shed their skin by rubbing themselves against rough surfaces. Though they shed their skin to grow, moulting also helps them get rid of the parasites living on their skin.

▲ *A moulted snakeskin*

Behaviour

Snakes have sufficiently developed intelligence. They are quite adaptive and some can even be tamed. They are deceptive in their appearance. Many a time, non-poisonous snakes look more dangerous than the poisonous ones. All snakes are carnivorous. They feed on a variety of animals from spiders to rats.

Locomotion

Amazingly, snakes do not have legs. They move from one place to another by crawling. Generally, they crawl by pushing themselves against the ground to move forward. Snakes with heavier bodies crawl with the help of their ribs.

Facts

- Bull snakes, often known as harmless snakes are named so because they make sounds like the snorts and grunts of a bull.
- Snakes can survive without food for almost 3-6 months.

How do snakes move from one place to another?

Venomous Snakes

Venomous snakes can inject the venom they produce into their prey. These snakes inject the venom with their specialized teeth, commonly known as fangs. They use their venom either to immobilize their prey or as a weapon for self-defence.

Mambas

Mambas are known for the speed at which they can travel. They are found in various parts of Africa. Black Mamba is the longest venomous snake after the King Cobra. The Eastern Green Mamba and the Western Green Mamba are two other species of mamba. These species are primarily arboreal, while the Black Mamba is terrestrial. The bite of a green mamba can be fatal.

▼ *A King Cobra*

Cobras

Cobras are venomous snakes found in parts of Africa and Asia. There are about 30 species of cobras. The King Cobra, which is found in South and Southeast Asia is the longest venomous snake. It can reach a length of 5.5 meters. A single bite from a king cobra can deliver enough venom to kill 20 people.

> What are fangs?

Rattlesnakes

Rattlesnakes get their name from the rattle they have at the tip of their tail. These snakes are one of the most venomous snakes in the world. They are born with fangs that can inject venom, and can control the amount of venom they inject into their prey. Their bite can be life-threatening to humans if immediate help is not provided. However, rattlesnakes are likely to flee rather than attack a human.

▲ *A Mojave rattlesnake*

Facts

- The venom of a rattlesnake can kill its prey in 20 seconds.
- King cobras are the only snakes in the world that build nests for their young ones.

Boas and Anacondas

Boas and anacondas, also known as constrictors are huge non-poisonous snakes that kill their prey by strangling them. They are among the most primitive snakes.

Green and yellow

The largest snake in the world, the green anaconda can grow up to a length of 8.8 m long and weigh up to 227 kg. Green anacondas are mainly nocturnal and spend most of their time swimming and floating in the water. They usually feed on fish, birds, mammals and reptiles. The yellow anaconda is not as large as the green anaconda. It is usually found in the Brazilian wetlands of Pantanal and feeds on wading birds, fish and small mammals.

Behaviour

Boas and anacondas are solitary snakes. They are active at night and bask during the day. These snakes prefer to live in water rather than on land. Boas tend to hide in burrows dug by medium-sized mammals, while anacondas hide in the water.

Boa constrictors

Despite their size, boa constrictors are rather modest compared to other large snakes. Female boas are larger than males and can grow up to 3 m long. These snakes are found in Central America, South America and on some islands in the Caribbean. They are light brown, green, red or yellow in colour and have skin patterns. Their colour often helps them blend in with their surroundings.

Anacondas

Anacondas are typically found in tropical South America. They can move both on land and in water. They have very strong muscles all over their bodies that help them move around. Anacondas are good swimmers and efficient climbers.

What do green anacondas eat?

Facts

- A group of anacondas is called a 'bed' or a 'knot'.
- Anacondas and boas swallow their prey whole and can survive for weeks or months without food after a large meal.

A man pulling a green anaconda ▶

Pythons

Pythons are thick-bodied, non-venomous snakes found in Asia, Africa and Australia. Like boas and anacondas, pythons are also constrictors. They kill their prey by squeezing them tightly and swallowing them whole. There are 32 species of pythons, most of which are native to the tropics.

▲ *A reticulated python*

Reticulated pythons

These gigantic pythons are one of the longest snakes in the world and can grow up to 8.7 m long. Reticulated pythons are native the rainforests, grasslands and forests of Southeast Asia. They are excellent swimmers and usually prefer to live near waterbodies. Although they do not prey on humans, reticulated pythons can easily kill a human by constricting them.

Burmese pythons

Burmese pythons have beautiful patterns on their skin. They are among the largest snakes, reaching up to a length of 7 m or more. They can weigh up to 90 kg. They are good swimmers and can stay underwater for up to 30 minutes before surfacing for air.

Green pythons

Green pythons are found in regions of New Guinea, Indonesia and Cape York Peninsula in Australia where they inhabit rainforests, bushes, trees and shrubs. Green pythons are arboreal species. Adult green pythons have a striking yellow or green coloured body. However, the hatchlings are of a yellow colour with irregular stripes and spots of purple and brown, gold, or red or orange.

How do pythons kill their prey?

Facts

- Baby, a Burmese python living at the Serpent Safari Park in Illinois, is the heaviest (183 kg) living snake.
- Pythons are known to snatch chickens, cats and dogs from areas near human habitation.

Sea Snakes

Sea snakes are marine snakes that live in water. Most sea snakes are found in the waters of the Indian and Pacific oceans. Although they are descended from terrestrial ancestors, sea snakes cannot survive on land. However, as they do not have gills, they regularly come to the surface to breathe. Sea snakes are poisonous.

What do they look like?

Sea snakes have a flattened, paddle-like tail that allows them to swim easily underwater. Unlike other reptiles, most sea snakes are able to breathe through their skin. They usually remain calm and only show aggression when attacked.

Extremely venomous

Although sea snakes are highly venomous, they inject very little venom when they bite. Their bites are usually painless and cause little or no swelling. However, because the bites often go unnoticed, they can cause severe damage such as rapid breakdown of skeletal muscle tissue and paralysis. Initial symptoms of sea snake bites include generalised aching, stiffness of all muscle groups and pain with passive muscle stretching.

Feeding and reproduction

Sea snakes feed mainly on fish. Occassionally, they may also eat fish eggs. Sea snakes that live in reefs have a small head and a thin neck that allows them to feed on small eels. Sea snakes lay their eggs inside their body. When the eggs are ready to hatch, they give birth to their young in the water.

What helps sea snakes to swim underwater easily?

Facts
- Sea snakes can swallow a fish more than twice the size of their neck.
- Yellow sea snakes are the longest of all sea snakes.

The World of Tortoises

Tortoises are slow-moving terestrial reptiles that have a hard bony carapace, commonly known as shell. There are about 40 species of tortoises. Tortoises inhabit various types of warm habitats, from deserts and semi-arid areas to tropical forests.

Birth

Tortoises are egg-laying reptiles. Female tortoises lay eggs at night in a burrow or nest dug in the sand. They can lay up to 30 eggs at a time. The incubation period is between 60 to 120 days, depending upon the species. The temperature of the nest determines the sex of an egg. Warm temperatures favour the birth of female tortoises and cold temperatures favour the birth of male tortoises. Once hatched from the egg, a tortoise lives on its own.

Diet

Tortoises are herbivorous reptiles. They feed on a variety of plants, flowers and grasses. However, the diet of a baby tortoise differs from that of an adult tortoise. Since a baby tortoise needs more nutrition, it is a carnivore. For instance, it consumes worm and insect larvae to get extra protein.

Lifespan

Tortoises have a long lifespan. They can live from 100 to 250 years. Adwaita, who died at the age of 255, is the longest-lived tortoise. Tui Malila (188 years) and Harriet (175 years) are the other two with the longest life span after Adwaita.

▲ *An African tortoise*

Which was the longest-lived tortoise?

Facts

- The size of the eggs depends on the size of the mother.
- Tortoises are found in every continent except Antarctica.

Giant Tortoises

Giant tortoises, as their name suggests, are huge in size. They can grow to be more than 1.3 m long and weigh up to 300 kg. These huge tortoises are found on the tropical islands of Madagascar, the Seychelles island, Mauritius, Réunion, the Galápagos, Sulawesi, Timor, Flores and Java.

Evolution

Giant tortoises belong to an ancient group of reptiles. They have been around for 2 to 3 million years. These giant tortoises were on the verge of extinction in 1900. In those times, the sailors used to hunt them for food.

Aldabra giant tortoises

Aldabra giant tortoises, found in the Aldabra atoll in the Seychelles islands are one of the largest tortoises in the world. They have a brown or tan, dome-shaped carapace and a long neck, which they often use to reach out to the tree branches that are high above the ground. Aldabra giant tortoises usually feed on fruits and vegetation. However, some occassionaly feed on carrion.

African spurred tortoises

African spurred tortoises are found along the southern edge of the Sahara Desert, North Africa. They are the third largest species of tortoise. Although it is assumed that these tortoises can live up to 80 years, the longest-living African spurred tortoise was 56 years old.

Which is the largest tortoise in the world?

Galápagos tortoises

Galápagos tortoises are the largest living tortoises in the world. These slow-moving reptiles are found on the Galápagos Islands in the Pacific Ocean. Fully-grown Galápagos tortoises can weigh up to 300 kg and extend up to 1.5 m in length (across the shell). These tortoises feed on cacti, grasses, leaves and fruits. Their preferred food is fresh young grasses. Due to massive hunting in the 19th century, these tortoises have become endangered.

Facts

- Chersobius signatus, also known as speckled Cape tortoises are the smallest tortoises.
- The Réunion giant tortoise, which was native to the Réunion Island in the Indian Ocean, is an extinct species of giant tortoises.

Freshwater Turtles

Turtles are the cousins of land tortoises and live in aquatic habitats. Like tortoises, they also have a carapace. However, their carapace is not always bony like that of tortoises. It can also be leathery. Depending on their habitat, turtles can be classified as freshwater and sea turtles.

Small turtles

Freshwater turtles are small turtles that live in flowing water. These turtles usually do not venture out of their watery homes. Most species of freshwater turtles are small with a few exceptions.

Alligator snapping turtles

Alligator snapping turtles are the largest freshwater turtles in North America. They get their name from the spiked shell, beak-like jaws and thick, scaled tail, which gives them an alligator-like appearance. They are also known as the 'dinosaurs of the turtle world'. These turtles are commonly found in the waters of the southeastern United States.

> Which turtle is known as the 'dinosaur of the turtle world'?

Common snapping turtles

The common snapping turtle is a large freshwater turtle found in Mexico, southeastern Canada, the mountains of western North America, and in Ecuador. These turtles are also referred to as snapping turtles. They are the largest freshwater turtle in the western United States. They are hunted for their meat and are widely used in turtle soup.

Facts

- Alligator snapping turtles lure their prey by excreting a red worm-like meat that attracts many fish.
- Musk turtles, which are found in the eastern United States are freshwater turtles known for the unpleasant musky odour they give off when disturbed.

▼ An African helmeted turtle

Sea Turtles

Sea turtles are found in all the seas of the world except the Arctic. They spend most of their time submerged in their marine habitats and only come to the surface to breathe. All the species of sea turtles are endangered.

Adaptations

Sea turtles have several adaptations that help them survive. They have a streamlined body and large flippers, instead of feet, which help them survive in their aquatic habitat. Sea turtles have the ability to breathe anaerobically. Another important adaptation is the salt glands in the corner of their eyes, nostrils or tongue, which they use to excrete excess salt.

Seven species

There are seven species of sea turtles:

- Flatback
- Hawksbill
- Leatherback
- Olive Ridley
- Green turtle
- Kemp's Ridley
- Loggerhead

Lifestyle

Sea turtles can live up to 80 years. Although they live in the ocean, they lay their eggs on land. The female turtles come out of the water and dig a nest in the sand. In this nest they lay their eggs. The nests are about 40–50 cm deep. Female turtles can lay 50–200 eggs at a time depending on the species. In general, the incubation period for sea turtles is about two months.

> Which is the largest sea turtle?

Leatherbacks

Leatherbacks are the largest species of sea turtles. They can grow up to 2 m long and weigh up to 900 kg. Unlike other turtles, leatherback turtles have a soft, cartilaginous shell rather than a hard, bony one. They are great swimmers and divers and are known for the long migrations they make.

Facts

- The largest leatherback was a male turtle that was 2.6 m long and weighed 916 kg.
- The Moche people of ancient Peru worshipped the sea and all its animals.

▼ *A sea turtle wading through the ocean*

Worm Lizards

Worm lizards, also known as amphisbaenians, are found in Africa and South America. A few of them are also found in other parts of the world. They are members of the lizard family, but bear an outward resemblance to Earthworms. Like Earthworms, worm lizards have a cylindrical body and live in burrows in the soil.

Behaviour

Not much is known about the behaviour of worm lizards since most members of this species remain underground. They are carnivores and feed on Earthworms, spiders and insects. They crawl by moving their skin forward, which is loosely attached to the body. As the skin moves, the body too is dragged along it.

What do they look like?

Worm lizards have an elongated and cylindrical body. They lack external ears and their eyes are covered with skin and scales. They do have hind limbs, and many of them lack forelimbs as well. They can grow up to around 30 cm long. They have a strong head merged with their neck. Their head is either round and oblique or oblique with a ridge in the middle.

Florida worm lizards

Florida worm lizards are found only in the United States in the regions of north and central Florida. Some of them are also found in southern Georgia. They are found in the sand-hills and oak trees present in the region. They are pinkish-white in colour and lack legs. They have rings around their bodies, like Earthworms.

A worm lizard digging a burrow in the soil. ▼

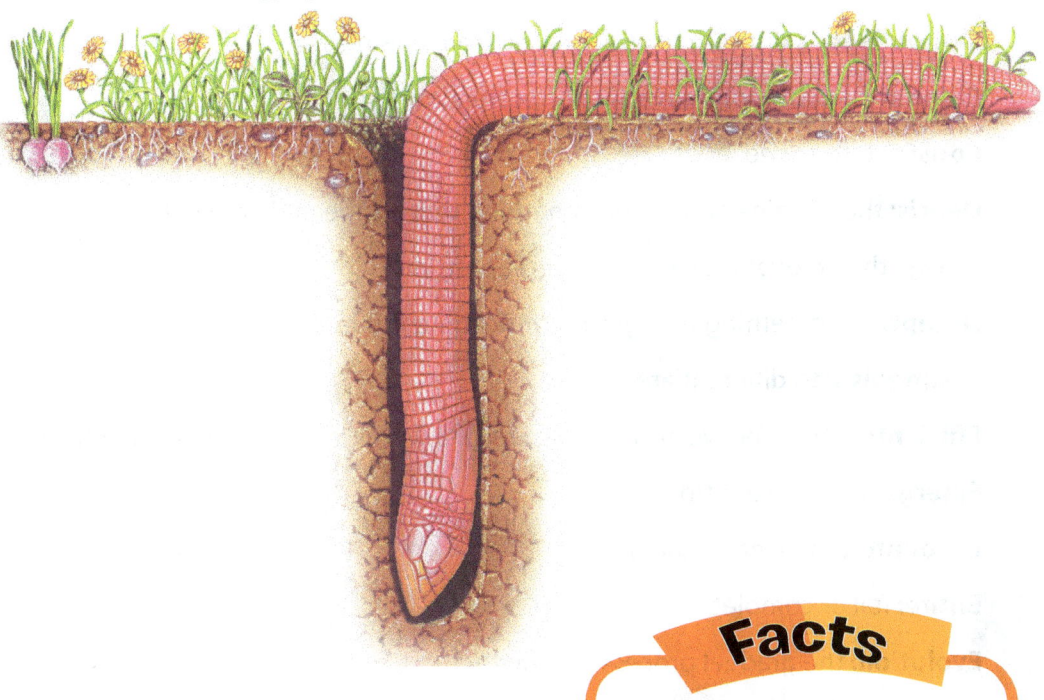

Facts

- Mexican mole lizards are worm lizards that have only two legs, each with five toes.
- Worm lizards can also move their skin and body backwards.

What is the colour of a Florida worm lizard?

Glossary

Adapt: to become suitable for a particular environment

Aggressive: ready to attack

Ancient: very old

Appearance: physical outlook

Arboreal: living in trees

Camouflage: a disguise to save oneself from enemies

Carapace: a hard bony covering for protection

Constrict: to squeeze

Debris: the remains or ruins of something that has been destroyed

Decay: the gradual process of ruining or rotting

Deceptive: something that gives a misleading impression

Distinguish: to differentiate

Efficient: to be effective and produce results without wasting time and effort

Emerge: to come out from

Encounter: to meet by chance

Entire: full or complete

Evolution: the gradual process of growth

External: an outer part of something

Fatal: causing death

Habitat: the natural environment in which an organism lives

Hatchling: a baby that has emerged from an egg

Immobilize: to make something stationary

Inject: the act of introducing liquid into the body

Insectivore: an animal or plant that eats only insects

Mystery: something that cannot be explained, or a secret that raises curiosity

Ornament: a decorative item used to beautify something or make it attractive

Parietal eye: a third eye found in the middle part of the brain and is covered by skin

Piranha: a small carnivorous freshwater fish with sharp teeth found in south america

Primitive: relating to an early stage in the development of something

Propel: to go forward

Projectile tongue: a long tongue that can be shot from the mouth to catch the prey

Resemble: to look like something or someone

Restrict: to limit or confine

Severe: very serious, intense

Snout: the projecting nose and mouth of an animal

Solitary: to live alone or be lonely

Sufficient: as much as needed or enough quantity

Suffocate: to choke or hamper the breathing process of an organism

Symptom: a sign or trait of a disease

Answers

Page No. 9   the saltwater crocodile found in Australia

Page No. 11   30–60 eggs

Page No. 13   Because they have narrow jaws

Page No. 15   Monitor lizard

Page No. 16   Veiled chameleons

Page No. 19   Galápagos Islands

Page No. 21   Reticulate Gila monster and banded Gila monster

Page No. 23   Once in four years

Page No. 25   By crawling

Page No. 26   Specialized teeth in snakes that inject venom

Page No. 29   Fish, birds, mammals and reptiles

Page No. 31   By constricting

Page No. 33   A paddle-like tail

Page No. 35   Adwaita

Page No. 36   Galápagos Tortoise

Page No. 38   Alligator snapping turtle

Page No. 40   Leatherback

Page No. 43   Pinkish-white

INSECTS AND SPIDERS

Introduction

Insects and spiders are some of the most interesting creatures in the world. They can fly and crawl. They live on land, in ponds and oceans. From ants to bumblebees, crabs to crayfish, spiders to centipedes all belong to the family of arthropods. They are the largest group of animals on Earth. Despite this unbelievable diversity, the basic body plan of arthropods is fairly constant. Arthropods are animals with segmented bodies that are formed by three units—head, thorax and abdomen.

They are cold-blooded invertebrates with six or more jointed legs. They vary in size from being as small as ants to being as huge as giant crabs. All arthropods have a hard armour-like exoskeleton which protects their delicate bodies. Their bodies grow as they mature but the exoskeleton does not, and so they undergo moulting at every stage of their life till they become completely mature.

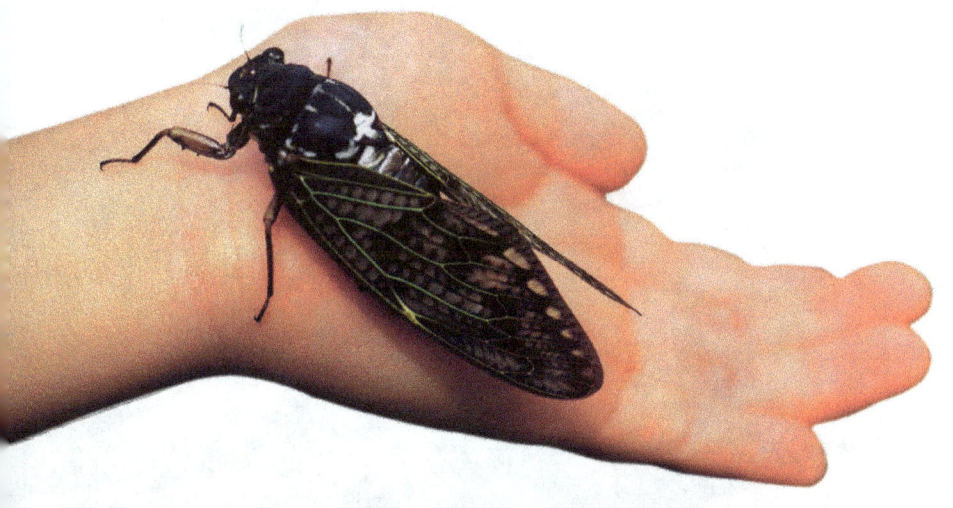

Evolution of Insects and Spiders

Evolution is a process by which different types of living organisms have developed from their earlier forms. Evolution may occur when there are changes in the characteristic traits within a population. Insects and spiders are believed to have evolved from marine crustaceans. Crustaceans are a large primitive group of arthropods. The evolution of spiders and insects dates back to 400 million years ago (early Devonian Period).

Where did insects come from?

Large winged insects were found during the Carboniferous Period (320-350 million years ago). During this period, insects diversified and assumed several different forms. Giant cockroaches and dragonflies having a wingspan of 50–70 cm were common during this period. However, several of these forms became extinct during the mass extinction that occurred 65 million years ago. The insects that survived the mass extinction greatly reduced in size. These insects were the ancestors of modern-day insects.

Where did spiders come from?

Spiders have evolved from trigonotarbids. Trigonotarbids were a group of ancient spiders that did not have spinnerets. They walked on eight legs and respired through book lungs like modern spiders. Also, they were terrestrial and lived in fern forests. However, they became extinct during the Early Permian Period.

Where was the Rhyniognatha hirsti fossil found?

Facts

- The oldest insect fossil is that of Rhyniognatha hirsti, which is more than 396 million years old. It was found in the Rhynie Chert rock in Scotland, Europe.
- Trigonotarbids are the oldest known land arthropods.

Habitat

A habitat is the natural environment where a plant, animal or any other organism lives. To retain its health and its inhabitants, the habitat of any species should not be overpopulated or lack in food or shelter. Animals and plants are adapted to the conditions of their habitats.

Spiders and their habitat

Spiders live in almost every nook and corner of Earth, barring the polar regions, the highest mountains and oceans. Spiders are travellers and often allow the direction of the wind to choose their habitat. They release silk threads that are caught by the wind, carrying them up and away. Some land close by while others may travel long distances across land or sea. At times, certain species may become isolated in a particular place due to climate change or rising sea levels. These isolated populations have to adapt to specialized habitats and may not be able to survive outside them.

Loss of habitat

European butterflies, beetles, dragonflies, damselflies and many other insects are suffering from the loss of habitat due to climate change, logging and depletion of freshwater sources. Their populations are declining, and many of them are faced with the risk of extinction. Nine per cent of the European butterflies, 11 per cent of the saproxylic beetles and 14 per cent of the dragonflies are threatened with extinction due to habitat loss.

Insects and their habitat

Insects are adapted to staying in environments most suitable to them—where they find food in plenty and can reproduce. Many insects decompose plant matter and are typically found in soil, leaf litter or rotting logs. Many unique species of butterflies and moths are found in the tropical regions of the world. Aquatic insects such as mayflies and dragonflies are found near water, marshes, ponds, lakes and streams. Insects like fleas and lice can be found on the bodies of animals. Arboreal insects such as bees and wasps can be found on flowers or in foliage.

Facts

- Thought most insects are solitary, some social insects such as bees, ants and termites live in large colonies.
- Twenty-nine beetle species that are only found only in Europe are threatened with global extinction.

Can spiders survive the chilly weather of polar regions?

Insect Body

Insects form the largest group in the animal kingdom. Their body is divided into three parts: head, thorax and abdomen. They have three pairs of jointed legs and a pair of antennae.

Head

The head of an insect supports a pair of antennae, a pair of eyes and external mouthparts. Insects can have two types of eyes—single or compound. Compound eyes are usually large with many lenses, whereas single eyes contain only one lens. The head is the most powerful part of an insect's body.

Thorax

The middle part of an insect's body is known as the thorax. It contains all the three pairs of legs, wings and muscles that control movement. The wings of insects are supported by thick veins, whose pattern varies from one insect to the other.

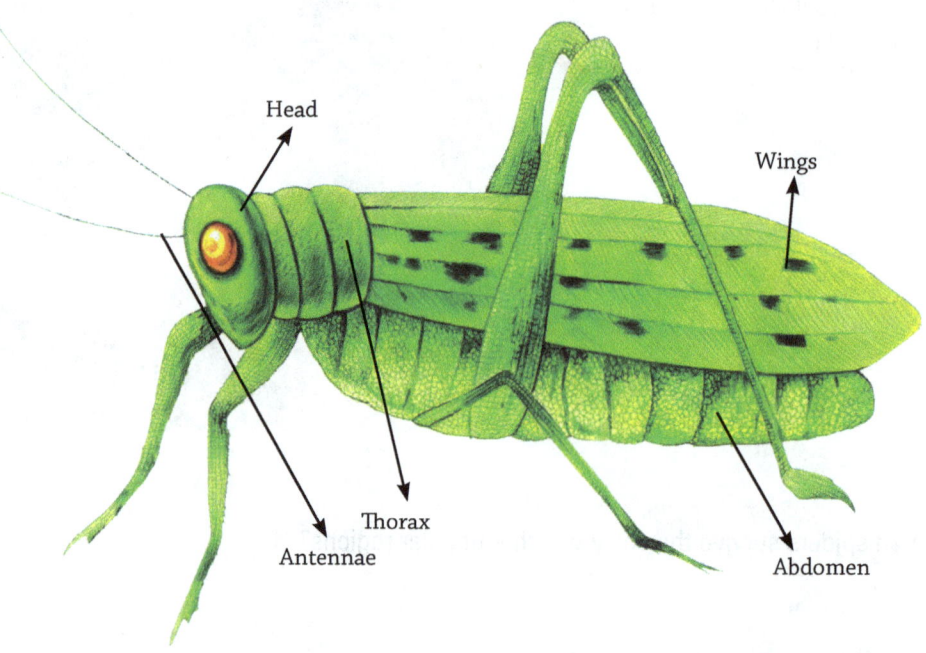

Organs and senses

The nervous system of an insect consists of the brain, which is formed by the fusion of three pairs of ganglia. A ganglion is a collection of neurons or nerve cells. The pairs of ganglia absorb nutrients from the food an insect eats and supports growth by providing it energy. Tympanal organs located on different parts of the body, such as wings, the abdomen, legs and antennae, help insects in hearing. In some insects such as bees, wasps and ants, antennae may contain the taste organs. The sense of touch is extremely important to insects and they use modified forms of sensory detectors to detect changes in temperature and Earth's magnetic field.

Abdomen

The abdomen contains all the vital organs including the respiratory, excretory, digestive and reproductive systems. The abdomen can expand when the insect feeds. It is also the most recognisable part of an insect's body.

The ganglion is a collection of _____.

Facts

- Some insects have both simple and compound eyes.
- Many insects can detect particular odours that are miles away from their location.

Life Cycle of Insects

All the stages in the life of an organism make up its life cycle. It begins with the birth of an organism that passes through several stages before becoming an adult. The lifecycle ends with the death of the organism. All living organisms, including insects and arachnids, go through several life stages.

Eggs

Insects begin life as eggs. The outer covering of the egg—the chorion—contains a spongy layer of air spaces that allow the exchange of gases, helping the embryo to breathe. Depending on the species of insects, the embryo may take a few days or as long as months to develop inside an egg. Once it is fully developed, the chorion breaks open and the insect emerges.

Nymphs

Some insects experience gradual metamorphosis and enter the nymph stage after they emerge from their eggs. Nymphs live in the same habitat as adults and eat the same kind of food. They mostly resemble adults, but their wings and genitals are yet to be formed completely. This stage is characterized by moulting—shedding of the exoskeleton. With each moult, nymphs grow further by developing wings and increasing in size. Finally, they have the same mouthparts as adults and also eat the same kind of food.

Larvae

Some insects experience complete metamorphosis and enter the larval stage after they emerge from their eggs. Like nymphs, larvae also experience moulting. During this stage, a new exoskeleton replaces the old one. The new skeleton is soft and expandable, which helps to accommodate further growth. In some insect species, there are very few changes at this stage, but some species such as butterflies experience great changes. When a fully-grown larva moults, it becomes a pupa.

Pupae and adults

The pupa stage includes major changes, which is often called metamorphosis. The pupa has almost the same shape as the adult. However, the pupal case or cocoon encloses its head, legs and wings. The insects wrap themselves into cocoons where they develop over time. Once they emerge from the cocoons, they enter adulthood. At this stage, the insects stop moulting.

Facts

- A maggot is a special kind of fly larva that has a small pointed head and is legless. It can be found in decaying matter.
- While most insects lay their eggs, some female cockroaches, bugs and flies carry the eggs in their body till they hatch.

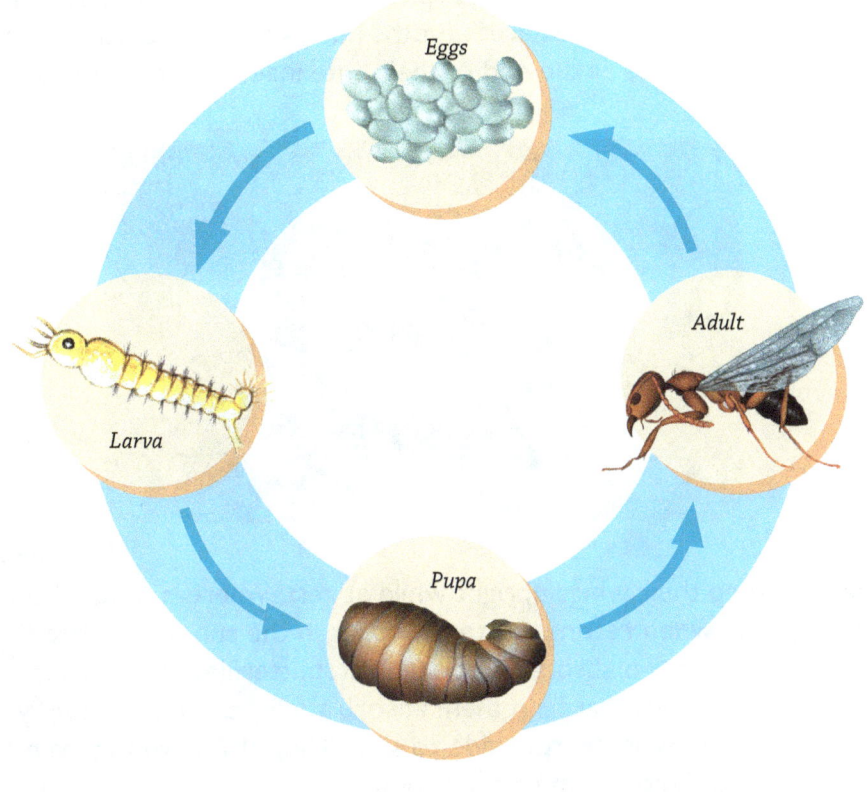

What is the outer covering of an insect egg called?

Butterflies and Moths

Butterflies and moths live in every part of the world, though some species live only in a small area. Butterflies are usually bright-coloured and diurnal creatures, whereas moths are dull-coloured, and they fly and feed at night. Both of them have large, scaly wings and their scales form different patterns on the wings.

Physical characteristics

Both butterflies and moths have a long, tube-like tongue called a proboscis, which they use for sipping nectar and other juices. They feed on flower nectar, tree sap, rotten fruit, animal dung, bird droppings, etc. They smell with the help of their antennae and breathe through openings in their abdomen and thorax called spiracles. Butterflies have large eyes and a keen sense of sight, whereas moths have sharp sensory receptors. Butterflies have knobs at the end of their antennae, whereas moths do not have such knobs.

Behaviour

Butterflies keep their wings upright while at rest, whereas moths keep their wings flat when resting. Butterflies bask in the sun to regulate their body temperature. To absorb more sunlight, butterflies usually have dark-coloured bodies that help them absorb sunlight. They do not fly in a straight line and wobble from side to side. They also have tiny hair on their feet, which helps them to taste food.

Monarch butterflies

Monarch butterflies are large butterflies with a wingspan of 10–13 cm. They have distinct orange, black and white markings on their wings. Unlike other butterflies or moths that live for one to a few weeks, monarch butterflies tend to live for about 9 to 10 months. These butterflies are popularly known for their seasonal migration. Each year during fall, monarchs living in Canada and the US begin their journey towards the South. They cover more than 3,200 km and reach central Mexico or Southern California.

Which is the largest moth in the world?

Facts

- Atlas moths are the largest moths in the world.
- There are about 15,000 to 20,000 butterfly species in the world.

Bees

Bees are flying insects that produce honey and beeswax. Around 20,000 species of bees are known to humans, though the actual number may be higher. Bees play an important role in the pollination of flowering plants and gathering nectar. They belong to one of the largest orders of insects.

What do they look like?

Bees have short and thick bodies. Their thorax has three segments, each attached to a pair of legs. They have two pairs of wings—the front and back wings are attached and appear like one. Bees use their antennae for smelling fragrances. They don't have ears—they sense the vibrations of surfaces where they sit. Bees move rapidly and their movement produces a humming sound. They fly at a speed of 20 km per hour, though they can fly much faster.

Classes

There are three classes of bees:
Worker bees: They are the smallest bees and they feed the drones and larvae. Worker bees have glands that produce wax, which they shape into the comb. They leave the hive to collect water, nectar and pollen.
Drones: They are the male bees. Their eyes are very large as compared to other bees. The only responsibility that drones have in the hive is to mate with the queen.
Queen bee: This is the largest bee in the hive. It mates with the drones only once in her life and lays eggs. Worker bees are responsible for feeding the queen bee.

Wasps

Bees and wasps are closely related to each other. They may look similar from a distance, but a closer observation would reveal the difference between them. Bees have robust bodies and are hairy, whereas wasps have slender and smooth bodies. Bees feed nectar and pollen to their young ones, whereas wasps are predators. They feed arthropods, flies and caterpillars to their young ones. Their sleek bodies make them good hunters. Bees use wax cells to make their nests in tree cavities, buildings or holes in the ground. Wasps use a papery pulp to make their nests. They prepare the pulp with chewed-up fibres and their saliva.

Facts

- When the honeybee stings, its stinger that is attached to the digestive system rips off the body. This causes the death of the honeybee immediately after it stings.
- The largest bees could be around 4 cm long. Some of the leafcutter and carpenter bees are the largest.

How many bee species are known to us?

Ants

Ants are social insects that belong to the same family as wasps and bees. Ants are believed to have evolved from wasp-like ancestors and they diversified after the rise of flowering plants. Ants are found almost everywhere in the world, but they are more commonly found in regions with hot climates.

Body

An ant's body is made of three parts—head, trunk and rear. They are often confused with termites as the two look very similar. Ants have six legs attached to the trunk and a pair of antennae on the head that help them hear, taste, touch and smell. They feed on fungi and dead bodies of other insects and especially like to eat sweets. Some even prey on reptiles, birds or small mammals. Ants breathe through tiny holes all over their body as they lack lungs.

Communication

Ants communicate with each other using chemical signals called pheromones. The antennae provide information about the direction and intensity of scents, hence they leave trails on the soil surface so that other ants can follow it.

Colonies

Ant colonies are well-structured nest communities located underground, in ground–level mounds or in trees. Each colony has three types of ants—queen, female workers and males, with some species having many queens. Female workers do not have wings and only the queen ant can lay eggs. The work of the males is limited to helping the queen reproduce and they do not live long after that. Soldier ants protect the queen, defend the colony and gather food. Each ant colony has a distinctive smell that helps them identify intruders.

Name the three types of ants in a colony.

Facts

- Ants can lift over 50 times their body weight.
- There are more that 12,000 species of ants in the world.

Beetles

Beetles represent almost one-fourth of the animal population. Interestingly, despite their small size, beetles are the strongest animals in the animal kingdom. They are found in every nook and corner of Earth feeding on living plants, rotting plants, animals (dead or alive) and animal waste.

Wings

Beetles are similar to other insects in all physical aspects except for their wings. They have four wings, of which only the ones at the back are used for flying. Being thin, beetles need their front wings for protection. Therefore, their front wings have evolved into hard covers. They are thick and opaque and do not have veins like those used for flying. They have to lift their front wings out of the way to fly.

Ladybugs

Ladybugs, also known as lady beetles or ladybird beetles, have beautifully patterned bodies. The most famous among these pretty beetles is the seven-spotted ladybug, with a shiny red-and-black body. Ladybugs feed on aphids and other plant-eating pests. In many cultures, it is believed that these harmless creatures bring good luck.

Facts
- A ladybug can eat up to 5,000 insects in its entire life.
- A firefly is a beetle that glows in the dark.

How many wings do beetles have?

Rhinoceros beetles

Rhinoceros beetles, also known as rhino beetles, are the strongest among all beetles. They are named so due to the presence of horns in male beetles. They have a horn on the thorax and another pointing forward from the centre of the thorax. They use their horns for several purposes, including digging holes in the ground for a hideout. The main purpose of the horns, however, is to lift rivals and move them out of the way. Though rhino beetles are huge, they are potentially harmless to humans as they cannot bite or sting. These beetles are found in all the continents except for Antarctica.

Cockroaches and Termites

Cockroaches and termites belong to the same family. The characteristic features distinguishing the members of this order is their oval and flattened body, long antennae and long, slender legs. Both cockroaches and termites are social insects found in every part of the world except Antarctica.

Cockroaches

Cockroaches are one of the few insects that inhabit all the countries in the world. They are found in the hottest as well as the coldest regions of the globe. Cockroaches can survive on almost anything—cheese, glue, paper as well as human hair and fingernails. They spend most of their time in cracks and crevices near food and water sources. Cockroaches are disliked all around the world because they contaminate food and secrete an unpleasant odour. Their blood is white due to the lack of haemoglobin. They have a much higher radiation resistance as compared to humans.

Termites

Termites are familiar to almost every household around the world as wood-eating insects. They mostly feed on dead plant material from wood, leaf litter, soil and animal dung. Like bees, termites also form colonies containing nymphs, workers, soldiers and the egg-laying queen or at times queens.

Anthills

Termites stay in nests made by worker termites using soil, mud, chewed wood and saliva. Termite mounds, also known as anthills, occur when a nest above the ground grows beyond its initially concealed surface. Termites are weak insects and need protection from ants and other predators. They build shelter tubes from soil and their waste across surfaces to gain access to wood.

What is the colour of a cockroach's blood?

Facts

- Cockroaches can go without eating food for a month but can only live for a week without water.
- Cockroaches can swim and hold their breath for about 40 minutes.

Crickets, Locusts and Grasshoppers

Crickets, locusts and grasshoppers belong to the family of insects with straight wings. These insects undergo incomplete metamorphosis and are characterized by the sounds they produce to attract female insects. They make clicking sounds by rubbing their wings against each other or their legs.

Crickets

Crickets, also known as 'true crickets', are leaping insects found under rocks and logs in meadows, pastures and along roadsides. They have flattened cylindrical bodies with strong hind legs that help them in jumping. Although they have wings, most of them cannot fly. Crickets have an extraordinary sense of vision as they have compound eyes. This enables them to see in several directions at the same time. Their organs for hearing are located on their knees. Crickets are omnivorous scavengers that feed on decaying plant material, fungi and some seeding plants.

Locusts

Locusts are solitary insects that look similar to grasshoppers but have an entirely different lifestyle. Locusts are short-horned grasshoppers. These insects are famous for their catastrophic invasions. They can breed rapidly under suitable conditions, travel great distances and greatly damage crops. They occur in many parts of the world, but presently, locust swarms are most destructive in the agricultural regions of Africa.

Grasshoppers

Grasshoppers are herbivorous insects with long hind legs for hopping and short front ones for catching prey as they walk. They are found everywhere except the North and South Poles. Grasshoppers have two large compound eyes and three simple eyes, which enable them to see in all directions at once. It is very difficult to catch them due to their enhanced vision, and if they feel threatened, they excrete a brownish 'tobacco juice' from their mouth.

What do crickets feed on?

Facts

- Grasshoppers can leap up to 20 times the length of their body.
- A desert locust swarm can pack about 40–80 million locusts into less than one square km of area.

Arachnids

Arachnids are a group of animals that have eight legs with seven joints, a segmented body and a hard exoskeleton. Some of them breathe with the help of air tubes, while some have lungs. The large group of arachnids includes spiders, scorpions, harvestmen, sun spiders, ticks and mites.

Harvestmen

Harvestmen are called so because they are usually seen during the harvest season. They have a small body and extremely long legs, which is why they are commonly called, daddy longlegs. They are as small as 0.7cm. However, their leg span may be as long as 16 cm. They feed on aphids, caterpillars, Earthworms, flies, beetles, dead and decaying plant and animal matter.

Sun spiders

Sun spiders, known by various names such as camel spiders, wind scorpions and solifugids, are found in hot dry deserts. They have a pair of large pedipalps that can be easily mistaken as an extra pair of legs. Pedipalps are sensory organs that these creatures use to sense the world around them. Most species of sun spiders hunt at night. They are one of the top predators in the environment they inhabit.

Mites and ticks

Mites are about 0.4 to 3 mm long, whereas ticks are about 3 to 29 mm long. They live in soil and water and as parasites on animals and plants. Some mites eat leaves and crops and are considered agricultural pests. Ticks, on the other hand, are parasites that feed on the blood of other living organisms. They suck the blood of their host and fall off when they are full.

How many legs do arachnids have?

Facts

- A tick's abdomen can expand 10 times its normal size.
- Among all the animals on Earth, sun spiders have the biggest jaws as compared to their size.

Life Cycle of Spiders

Spiders are one of the most common arachnids in the world. They are one of the most abundant creatures on the planet. They are predators that feed on small insects and other invertebrates. There is only one spider species that is herbivore. Like every other animal on the planet, spiders too have a life cycle.

Eggs

After mating, female spiders lay their eggs in a ball-like egg sac. The egg sac contains hundreds and thousands of eggs. Some female spiders carry their egg sac with them, while some hide it in a safe place. It takes a couple of days for the spiderlings to hatch.

Spiderlings

Spiderlings look like their parents but are paler in colour. Some spiders, such as wolf spiders, care for their spiderlings. They carry their babies on their backs and feed them till they are old enough to catch prey. However, some spiders leave the spiderlings to live on their own. After hatching, spiderlings walk away or use ballooning to move from place to place. They climb up to the top of an object, such as a leaf or grass blade, from where they secrete silk threads into the wind. The wind carries spiderlings from a few feet to hundreds of miles away. This act is called ballooning.

What are baby spiders called?

Facts

- A spider cannot digest solid foods. It excretes digestive juices over its prey and then sucks it.
- There are more than 50,000 species of spiders in the world.

Moulting

To grow and increase their size, spiderlings shed their exoskeleton and form a new, larger one. A spiderling grows an exoskeleton, which it moults many times to become an adult. Some spiderlings moult about five to six times before becoming adults, while some moult throughout their lives.

Spider Webs

Spiders weave webs with the help of a silk-like substance called spinneret. They secrete the spinneret from their abdominal glands. However, not all spiders spin webs and many live in the ground in burrows.

Kinds of webs

There are many kinds of spider webs—orb webs, cobwebs, funnel webs, spiral webs, sheetwebs, etc. Usually, spiders are known by the kind of webs they weave. Orb webs are one of the most common webs. These webs are shaped as spiral lines and are flexible and resistant. Orb web spiders repair their webs once every day. Cobwebs, on the other hand, are messy, irregular in shape and sticky.

Decorated webs

Some orb-web spiders use decorations while weaving their webs. The decorations attract insects towards the web, which get entangled and stuck once they enter the web. The spiders then devour their prey. The decoration also acts as a warning sign to birds so that they stay away from the webs. The spiders can also use decorations as sunshades.

Funnel webs

Funnel webs appear like funnels and are made up of dry and non-sticky silk. Their webs have an entrance that appears like a tunnel. There are several silk 'trip lines' at the entrance. Spiders sit at the entrance waiting for prey to pass by and trip into the web. The tunnel leads to a burrow lined with silk.

Uses of a spider web

Spiders spin webs for several purposes such as trapping insects for food, moving from one place to another, nest building, protecting eggs, etc. They have to weave and mend their webs almost regularly. Spiders also eat their webs and recycle the silk to make new ones or amend the old ones.

Facts

- Spider webs contain blood-clotting qualities, which is why people used them as bandages to stop bleeding in the past.
- The smallest spider is the mygalomorph spider and is about the size of a pinhead.

Name any two types of webs that spiders make.

Tarantulas

Tarantulas are large spiders with hair on their body. They are found everywhere except Antarctica. Tarantulas especially live in warm climates and are commonly found in tropical, subtropical regions and deserts. There are more than 800 species of tarantulas in the world. These spiders have also become popular pets among arachnid enthusiasts.

Burrowers

Tarantulas make burrows in the ground with the help of strong legs and fangs. Sometimes, they choose to live in burrows already made by other animals. They line their burrows with silk. During the winters the silk lining keeps their burrows warm. Tarantulas hardly come out of their burrows, especially during the day since they are nocturnal animals. They usually feed on insects but can also eat larger animals such as frogs, toads and mice. After having a meal, they may not need to eat for a month.

Facts

- The Paloma dwarf found in Southern Arizona is the smallest tarantula in the world. It has a leg span of about an inch.
- The South Americans are known to eat roasted tarantulas.

Name the largest tarantula.

Goliath bird-eaters

The Goliath bird eaters are the largest tarantulas (the size of a dinner plate) that are found in the coastal rainforests of South America. They were named by some explorers who saw a tarantula feeding on a hummingbird. However, these spiders rarely eat birds. They have a leg span of about 30.4 cm and weigh about 70 g. Goliath bird-eaters make a loud noise by rubbing their bristles on their legs.

Hairy spiders

Tarantulas are very hairy creatures. They sense the world around them with the help of the hair all over their body. They even have barbed hair on their abdomen. When in danger, a tarantula rubs its abdomen and flings barbed hair on the enemy. These tiny hair can cause extreme pain and irritation when they touch the skin or get into the eyes or mouth of the enemy.

Unusual Spiders-I

Some spiders have certain unusual characteristics that set them apart from other spiders. Some spiders are known for their special techniques of catching prey, while others are known for building unique webs.

Darwin's Bark spiders

Darwin's Bark spiders are orb web spiders. They make one of the largest orb webs of all spider webs. One of the largest webs was discovered in 2009 in Madagascar that was 25 m wide. Recently, it has been discovered that Darwin's Bark spiders weave webs bridging the rivers in Madagascar.

Diving bell spiders

Diving bell spiders or water spiders live underwater throughout their lives. These spiders come to the surface to breathe air. They build bubble nests to live underwater and replenish their nests with air, which take up the shape of a bell. This is why they are called diving bells. They use their bubble webs to digest prey, moult, lay eggs and raise babies. The spiders come out of their nest to catch prey.

> Which spider hunts other spiders for food?

Facts

- Pirate spiders hunt and eat other spiders.
- Spider wasps sting trapdoor spiders and deposit their eggs on them. When baby spider wasps hatch, they gorge on the living spider.

Bola spiders

Bola spiders are easily recognisable due to their large abdomen. They have an unusual way of catching prey. These spiders spin a single line of silk that has a clump or ball (bola) of silk at the end. This is the reason they are called bola spiders. They swing, swirl and twirl the bolas in the air to attract insects. Moths are usually attracted to the smell of their silk and fly towards them only to be stuck. The spiders then roll in the silken thread to eat their prey.

Unusual Spiders-II

Among the 50,000 species of spiders present in the world, some spiders possess certain extraordinary qualities, which make them different from the others.

Jumping spiders

Jumping spiders are easily recognisable by the four pairs of prominent eyes at the top of their head. They also have four smaller eyes at the back of their head, which provide them with sharp vision. These spiders are called so because they can jump several times their own length. They use their jumping prowess to catch prey and avoid danger. They are active during the day.

Crab spiders

Crab spiders have flat, wide bodies and their two front pairs of legs are larger than the hind legs. They can walk sideways, forwards or backwards on their hind legs like crabs, which is why they are called crab spiders. They possess the ability to camouflage themselves according to their surroundings. They can change the colour of their body to match their surroundings, which can take a few days. They are passive hunters, which mean that they wait for their prey to come near them and then pounce on it.

Fishing spiders

Fishing spiders are found near water bodies. They have excellent vision and are capable of walking on the surface of water. They are amphibious in nature and can dive in water to feed on small fish, aquatic insects and tadpoles. This is why they are called fishing spiders. These spiders can even remain underwater for some time.

What does a fishing spider feed on?

Facts

- While moving and especially before jumping, a jumping spider releases a silk thread so that in case of a fall, it can climb up using the thread.
- Male jumping spiders dance before the females to show that they are interested in mating.

Venomous Spiders

Spiders are venomous creatures but the venom of a few spider species can be life-threatening to humans. A spider's venom glands are located near the fangs and it injects venom along with releasing digestive juices over a prey. There are three types of venom—neurotoxins, myotoxins and cardiotoxins.

Brown recluse spiders

Recluse spiders are also known as violin spiders, reapers and fiddle-back spiders. Unlike most spiders, recluse spiders have six equal-shaped eyes. The eyes are arranged in three pairs, which are called dyads. These spiders like to live in seclusion, which is why they are named recluse spiders. Brown recluse spiders are common recluse spiders. They are scavengers and prefer to feed on dead insects.

Funnel-web spiders

Funnel-web spiders are one of the most venomous spiders found in the coastal and mountainous regions of Australia. They make funnel-shaped webs, which is why they are called funnel web spiders. These spiders have small eyes that are closely grouped together, downward pointing fangs and hair on the abdomen. The venom of male funnel web spiders is more lethal than that of the females. The Sydney funnel web spider is the most venomous spider in Australia.

> Name a common widow spider.

Facts

- Female funnel web spiders may live for 20 years, whereas males live only for three to five years.
- Brown recluse spiders can live without food or water for about six months.

Widow spiders

Widow spiders are one of the most venomous spiders in the world. They are found everywhere in the world except Antarctica. Female widow spiders are known to kill and eat male widow spiders after mating. This is why they are called widow spiders. The black widow spider is one of the common widow spiders. It has a distinct red colouration on the underside of its belly. Its venom is a neurotoxin and is 15 times stronger than that of a rattlesnake.

Scorpions

Scorpions are about 13–18 cm long and are the largest arachnids. They are also the oldest known arachnids. They are found everywhere in the world except Antarctica. These predatory animals have been living on Earth since the era of dinosaurs. There are about 2,000 scorpion species in the world. The emperor scorpion is the largest of all scorpions.

Behaviour

Scorpions are burrowing animals that need loose soil to survive. These solitary animals can even kill another scorpion if it invades their territory. They stay in cool underground holes during the day and hunt at night. They feed on small insects, spiders, mice, lizards, etc. They kill their prey with venom filled in the stinger at the end of their tail. A scorpion grabs its prey with its claws and then raises its tail over its head to sting the prey.

Scorplings

A female scorpion gives birth to a litter of six to eight pale white scorplings at a time. The scorplings are born with a thin sheet of skin, which they break out of with the mother's help. Then they immediately climb onto their mother's back. The scorplings cannot survive without their mother's protection until have moulted at least once.

Special traits

Scorpions have a pair of grasping claws called pincers and a segmented tail ending in a stinger known as telson. They can survive in the harshest of conditions when food is scarce. Scorpions have the ability to slow down their metabolism rate and can live on only one insect per year.

- Scorpions have a pigment in their skin that makes them glow when exposed to ultraviolet light.
- Scorpions are believed to be the first animals that moved from water to land millions of years ago.

Scorpions hunt during the night. True/False?

Glossary

Amphibious: the ability to live both on land and in water

Catastrophe: an event that causes great harm and damage

Climate: the general weather conditions of a region over a long period

Concealing: hiding or covering from sight

Digestive juice: chemicals secreted by the stomach that help in digesting food

Distinctive: having special characteristics that makes something different from others

Diurnal: during the day

Exoskeleton: the hard outer covering of animals like that of insects

Gradual: taking place slowly

Intruder: someone who enters a place without permission

Invade: to enter a place forcefully and cause damage

Metamorphosis: the process by which the young ones of some animals develop into adults

Odour: smell

Opaque: through which light cannot pass

Parasite: an organism that takes nourishment from another organism

Pest: an insect or a small animal that harms crops and other plants

Pollination: the process by which pollen grains are transferred from the anther to the stigma

Predator: an animal that kills other animals for food

Prey: an animal that is hunted by another animal for food

Reproduce: to produce young ones through biological process, sexually or asexually

Robust: a strong and healthy built of body

Seclusion: to stay away from others of the same kind

Sensory: related to the physical senses

Solitary: to live alone

Spinneret: the organ in spiders and caterpillars that helps in making webs and cocoons

Trail: a mark, sign or scent left behind by an animal on its track

Ultraviolet light: a type of sunlight that is not visible to the naked eye but can cause sunburns

Venomous: containing venom or poison

Answers

Page No. 51	Scotland, Europe
Page No. 53	No
Page No. 55	Neurons or nerve cells
Page No. 57	Chorion
Page No. 59	Atlas moth
Page No. 61	20,000
Page No. 63	Queen, female workers and males
Page No. 64	Four
Page No. 67	White
Page No. 69	Decaying plant matter, fungi and some seeding plants
Page No. 71	Eight
Page No. 72	Spiderlings
Page No. 75	Cobwebs and funnel webs
Page No. 76	Goliath bird-eater
Page No. 78	Pirate spider
Page No. 81	Small fish, aquatic insects and tadpoles
Page No. 82	Black widow spider
Page No. 85	True

www.ingramcontent.com/pod-product-compliance
Lightning Source LLC
Chambersburg PA
CBHW050658160426
43194CB00010B/1985